HOMESTYLE
KOREAN COOKING
IN PICTURES

HOMESTYLE
KOREAN COOKING
IN PICTURES

By Cho Joong Ok

SHUFUNOTOMO/JAPAN PUBLICATIONS

Paper Over Board Edition
First printing: September 1991

Published by SHUFUNOTOMO CO., LTD.
2–9, Kanda Surugadai, Chiyoda-ku, Tokyo, 101 Japan

Sole Overseas Distributor: Japan Publications Trading Co., Ltd.
P.O. Box 5030 Tokyo International, Tokyo, Japan
Distributors:
UNITED STATES: Kodansha America, Inc., through Farrar, Straus &
Giroux, 19 Union Square West, New York, NY 10003.
CANADA: Fitzhenry & Whiteside Ltd., 195 Allstate Parkway, Markham,
Ontario L3R 4T8.
BRITISH ISLES AND EUROPEAN CONTINENT: Premier Book Marketing Ltd.,
1 Gower Street, London WC1E 6HA.
AUSTRALIA AND NEW ZEALAND: Bookwise International,
54 Crittenden Road, Findon, South Australia 5023.
THE FAR EAST AND JAPAN: Japan Publications Trading Co., Ltd.,
1–2–1, Sarugaku-cho, Chiyoda-ku, Tokyo 101.

ISBN 0–87040–502–0
Printed in Japan

Preface

Traditional Korean cooking came to the attention of the Western world only thirty years ago, when soldiers from sixteen countries came to fight in the Korean War. Soldiers on leave were able to sample the unique flavors in our dishes; and we like to think that after the war, when they returned to their own countries, memories of those exotic dishes occasionally flashed through their minds and evoked thoughts of the country for which they fought so bravely. Nowadays Korean cooking has a small but devoted band of enthusiasts among Westerners who have visited or lived in Korea.

Several years ago I published a booklet entitled *Korean Cooking* which attracted an unexpectedly wide audience and has been reprinted many times. The following pages are the result of many requests to publish a full length Korean cookbook in English. The recipes were selected for their universal appeal and for the availability of their ingredients. A few of the ingredients need to be purchased in Korean or other Oriental grocery stores, but many of the recipes can be prepared from food purchased at the local food store.

I wish to express my gratitute to the staff of Shufunotomo who encouraged me to publish *Home Style Korean Cooking in Pictures*, and to Mrs. Kimiko Nagasawa and Mrs. Laura Oberdorfer, who translated my Japanese text into beautiful English. It is my desire that through this book people of other lands will become lovers of Korean cooking.

Cho Joong Ok

Contents

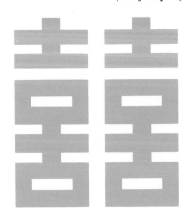

Korea, Confucianism, and Cooking

For many years feudalism and a family system based on Confucianism dominated the Korean people. During the long Li Dynasty, which was eastablished in 1392 and lasted for 27 generations until 1897, there were four social classes to which people belonged from birth: the privileged nobility, the intellectuals (engineers, interpreters, and lower government officials), the common people (farmers and businessmen), and the lowest class, despised by the others (slaves, craftsmen of musical instruments, priests, and Korean geisha). The living patterns of each class were rigidly set by regulations that affected people in every social activity.

The Korean family system which operated in all four classes was the mainstay of social order. Confucian morality ruled the relations between men and women, the old and the young in Korean families. Men were predominant over women in word and deed, and in matters of inheritance the rights of the elders had priority of those of the younger family members. This traditional family system has gradually given way with the modernization of Korean society, but remnants of it are still found in the country as the basis of social order.

The feudal system, which lasted until the end of the Li Dynasty, and the Confucian family system greatly affected the development of Korean cooking. (Indeed, their influence can still be seen today in the dietary customs of the people.) Two distinct types of cooking emerged: the cuisine of the royal court and the home cooking of the common people. The royal court cuisine is characterized by the use of a large variety of ingredients, a highly refined sense of seasonings and spices, elaborate cooking procedures, and elegant table settings. Distinguished and wealthy families today maintain the traditions of the court cuisine. Home-style cooking is less complex and elegant than that of the palace; it, too, is traditional, not having changed much since olden days.

Cooking and the Korean Housewife

The preparation of daily meals is one of the main activities of Korean housewives, for upholding the dietary customs is regarded as the responsibility of women.

One of these customs requires women to get up early in the morning, for the main meal of the day has traditionally been breakfast. Koreans like to fortify themselves before going off to work, instead of returning home tired at the end of the day to a heavy meal. The housewife can relax at lunch time, for the second meal of the day is usually quite simple. The word for lunch is *Jeomsim* 点心, which means "only to lighten your heart." (The tradition of the light lunch, incidentally, is one shared by both royal court cuisine and home-style cooking. During the days of the court, breakfast and dinner were formal affairs, but lunch consisted of only a plain dish of noodles or rice gruel mixed with red beans, peanuts, sesame seeds and pine nuts.)

Apart from business entertaining which is done in restaurants, Korean's traditionally prefer to entertain at home. Even full-scale banquets celebrating birthdays and weddings are given at home. The housewife's cooking abilities are put to the test on such occasions, with the result that home-style cooking has become a refined art of its own. Indeed, a Korean can tell the rank of a family from the variety and taste of the dishes devised and prepared by the women. With the reputation of the family at stake, cooking is indeed of the utmost importance to Korean housewives.

Festival, Ceremonial, and Special Dishes

There are many festivals in Korea based on the old lunar calendar. The food prepared for these festivals is appropriate to the season and is often symbolic. For example, on New Year's Day women spend much time preparing dishes to offer to the family ancestors as well as to the living members of the family. For the First Full Moon of the Year, people drink wine to prevent deafness and visit twelve houses during the day in each of which they are offered food to eat. A special rice dish containing plain rice, glutinous rice, millet, corn, and red beans is featured. At the beginning and in the middle of the dog days of summer, noodles are eaten for strength. And on the longest night of the year in winter, one eats only red bean gruel.

On happy family occasions such as weddings, the birth of a child, or the 61st birthday, a great feast of many dishes is formally served. The 61st birthday is important because the normal life span is considered to be 60 years and also because the cycle of years in the lunar calendar lasts for 60 years, after which one goes back to the beginning of the cycle. Thus, the 61-year-old is beginning a new cycle. (More details about feasts are given in the next section on Table Settings.)

The cuisine of the royal court is the basis for an elaborate à la carte presentation of foods called *Teuk-byeol Yori* or "Specialties." Many varieties of dishes characteristic of Korean cooking are included in the Specialties, ranging from hors d'oeuvres to rice cakes and cookies.

Korean Seasonings

Korean cooking gives high priority to nutrition as well as to taste. Believing that the hearty, everyday fare developed over the centuries can prevent and even cure illness, Koreans have continued to use traditional ways of cooking and adhered to the eating habits of their forefathers. It may well be that because they pay so much attention to the nutritious balance of foods, they generally look young for their age.

Characteristic of Korean cooking is a combination of five tastes (salty, sweet, sour, hot, bitter), an arrangement of five colors (red, green, yellow, white, black), and a diversity of ingredients generously seasoned before and after cooking. For example, the procedure for grilling beef is first to slice the meat thinly, then mix it with a sauce in which several seasonings and spices have been combined beforehand, then grill it, and at the table add more seasonings to taste.

The five tastes are found in the following ingredients:

1. Salty: Table salt, soy sauce, bean paste
2. Sweet: Sugar from beets, sweet potatoes, honey and maltose candy
3. Sour: Rice and citron vinegar
4. Hot: Red peppers, mustard
5. Bitter: Ginger

Several of these seasonings (soy sauce, bean paste, and vinegar) are usually made in the home.

Four of the five colors can easily be found in many different foods. To provide for the fifth color, black, Koreans add such things as cloud ear mushrooms.

Korean Spices

Spices are called 薬念 *Yang-nyeom*, meaning "to pray for virtue" because they are used partly to wish for health. Indispensable to the flavor of the dishes, spices and seasonings constitute the uniqueness of Korean cooking (in contrast to the cooking methods which are basically the same as in other countries). To a Korean, a dish without green onions, garlic, ginger, sesame seeds and oil—to name the most pervasive of the seasonings—is a dish without taste or savor.

Preparation of Korean Spices

1. Green onions: Usually minced, but sometimes cut into thin strips.
2. Garlic: Usually minced, but occasionally cut into thin strips. To intensify the flavor, crush cloves with the handle of knife before mincing.
3. Ginger: Usually minced, but sometimes thinly sliced or cut into thin strips. Crush in the same way as garlic.
4. Sesame seeds: Thoroughly wash and dry the fresh seeds to remove sand. Toast in a dry pan until they puff up; watch closely, for they burn easily. Grind.* Sometimes they are ground with a pinch of salt.
5. Dried red (or Chili) pepper: Ground; chopped or minced, after removing seeds; cut into very thin strips like threads as a garnish.**

*To grind sesame seeds, use a mortar and pestle (Oriental mortars are serrated on the inside), or a special sesame seed grinder available in Oriental grocery stores. If the sesame seeds are to be incorporated into a seasoning mixture containing soy sauce or other liquid, you can grind them in a blender, adding as needed the soy sauce to facilitate the process.

**Already prepared strips of dried red (or chili) pepper can be purchased in Korean grocery stores.

Black pepper, powdered cinnamon, and hot
Ask for red (or chili) pepper threads, or sliced
red (or chili) pepper.
mustard are other typical Korean spices. The preparation of hot mustard is described under Mixed Seasonings, below.

Mixed Seasonings

Mixed seasonings are added to the ingredients while cooking or are served as a dip. Each family has its own favorites, but the main ones are vinegar-soy sauce, vinegar-hot bean paste, and hot mustard.

Vinegar-Soy Sauce *(Cho Jang)*
Mix together 4 tablespoons soy sauce, 2 tablespoons vinegar, and 2 teaspoons lemon juice. Just before serving, sprinkle with 1 teaspoon finely chopped pine nuts.

Hot Bean Paste *(Kochu Jang)*
Mix together 2 tablespoons powdered red pepper, 2 tablespoons soy sauce, and 2 tablespoons bean paste. (A commercially prepared hot bean paste is available in Korean grocery stores; ask for Hot Sauce. A Chinese product called *tou-pan-chiang* is widely available and, though different from the Korean, is an adequate substitute.)

Vinegar-Hot Bean Paste *(Cho-Kochu Jang)*
Mix together 1 tablespoon hot bean paste, 2 tablespoons vineagr, and ½ teaspoon sugar.

Hot Mustard *(Kyeoja)*
Gradually stir 4–5 tablespoons lukewarm water or vinegar into 3 tablespoons mustard powder until it forms a thin paste.

Since there are no strict rules for making these mixtures, you may adapt them to your taste.

Base Recipes

Egg Decoration
Beat the required number of eggs with a little salt; beat lightly to avoid the formation of air bubbles and foam. Heat and oil a skillet (use vegetable or sesame oil), and fry eggs in very thin sheets. It is easier to work with a small skillet and make several egg sheets. When cool, cut the egg sheets into shreds or diamonds, as specified by the recipe. An easy way to shred an egg sheet is to roll it into a tube and cut across it.

Juice from the Giant White Radish
This is an ingredient in *Kimchi*, the Korean pickle. Grate the radish, then squeeze it through a loosely woven cotton dish towel or several layers of cheesecloth. Be sure to have a bowl underneath.

Toasted and Ground Sesame Seeds
Heat sesame seeds (the amount will be specified in the individual recipes), slowly in a dry pan. Watch carefully and remove from the heat as soon as they become brown and start to pop. Grind the seeds. (Asian grocery stores sell sesame seed grinders and Oriental mortars. The latter are serrated pottery bowls.)

Ingredients

Cloud Ears
A cup-shaped fungus with a crunchy texture.

Salted Shrimps
This is available in Korean grocery stores. It is called *Saewu-Jeot* in Korean, but if you ask for "Salted shrimp for *Kimchi*," the clerk will know what you mean. The tiny shellfish in this fermented seasoning are actually not shrimp at all but mysis, a small crustacean that closely resembles shrimp. *Saewu-Jeot* is used to season other dishes besides *Kimchi*—for example, the custard on p. 78.

Sul
Korean rice wine.

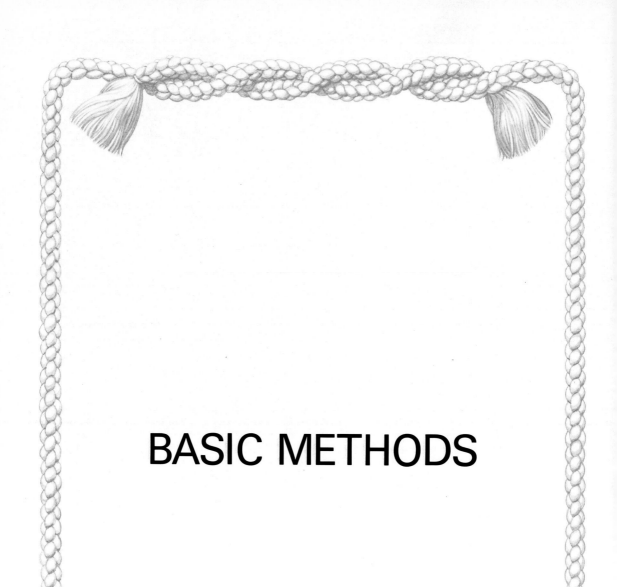

BASIC METHODS

Pickled Spring Garlic (*Maneul Jang-ajji*),
See page 79

Beef Soup (*Yangji Meori Komkuk*)

4 servings

Ingredients:

2 lb. (1 kg) beef (brisket or bottom round)
2 green onions, chopped
2 cloves of garlic, sliced
13 cups water
Seasoning Mixture:
  1 green onion, shredded
  1 tablespoon minced garlic
  3 tablespoons light soy sauce
  ½ tablespoon prepared sesame seeds (see recipe, p. 11)

⅓ teaspoon pepper
1½ tablespoons sesame oil
1 egg
A little salt
Dipping Sauce:
  1 tablespoon minced green onion
  1 teaspoon minced garlic
  ⅓ teaspoon pepper
  1 tablespoon sesame oil

Method:

1. Bring the water to a boil in a deep pan. Reduce heat and put in the beef. Remove scum thoroughly.
2. Add the green onions and garlic. Cover and simmer about 2½ hours. When broth is reduced by one-fourth, prick meat to see if it is cooked. Remove from pan and let cool for easy slicing. Strain the broth.
3. Thinly slice the meat. Combine ingredients for Seasoning Mixture and thoroughly mix with the sliced meat.
4. Return broth and meat to the pan. Bring to a boil and add salt to taste.
5. Make Egg Decoration (see recipe, p. 11). Shred finely.
6. Pour broth and meat into a tureen and garnish with the shredded Egg Decoration. Diners will need chopsticks (or forks) as well as soup spoons in order to dip the slices of meat into the Dipping Sauce.

Oxtail Soup (*Kkori Komkuk*)

4 servings

Ingredients:

2 lb. (1 kg) oxtail
13 cups water
Seasoning Mixture:
  2 green onions, chopped
  1⅓ tablespoons minced garlic
  3 tablespoons light soy sauce
  ½ tablespoon prepared sesame seeds (see recipe, p. 11)
  ⅓ teaspoon pepper
  2 tablespoons sesame oil
Salt and pepper

Method:

1. Chop oxtail into joints and wash well. Bring the water to a boil and add the meat. Remove scum thoroughly. Reduce heat and simmer about 3 hours. When a fork or skewer slides easily into meat, remove it and strain the broth.
2. Mix meat with Seasoning Mixture and return to the broth. Bring soup to a boil and add salt to taste.
3. Mix together salt and pepper and serve in a separate dish along with the soup. The diners can use the salt and pepper as a dip for the meat.

Tripe Soup (*Seolnong Tang*)

8 servings

Ingredients:
2½ lb. (1.2 kg) honeycomb tripe
1 lb. (500 g) beef bones (about 4-inches (10 cm) in all)
1 lb. (500 g) beef (brisket or bottom round)
Boiling water
2 green onions, chopped
Salt and pepper to taste

Method:
1. Wash the tripe and the beef bones. Place in a deep saucepan. Pour in enough boiling water to cover, and continue to boil over high heat.
2. When the surface is almost covered with scum, drain completely. Pour in enough fresh boiling water to cover, and cook over medium heat about 2 hours, skimming thoroughly.
3. Add brisket and continue to cook over low heat about 2 more hours, skimming occasionally. When the broth turns milky white, remove the bones.
4. When a skewer or fork slides easily into the tripe and brisket, remove from the broth. Slice thinly and return to the pot. Reheat to a boil before serving.
5. Serve with chopped green onions, salt and pepper.

Notes:
1. The fresh tripe that you buy in American butcher shops and supermarkets has already received considerable treatment: it has been thoroughly washed, scraped, and scalded to remove the inner stomach wall, and partially cooked before it leaves the packing house. However, if you buy tripe directly from a farmer, you will have to clean it yourself. First, immerse it in scalding water; boil it briefly, or let it sit in the water for 10 minutes. Next, scrape off the dark inner lining with a spoon, being careful not to break the white surface underneath. Finally rub the tripe under cold water, and rinse many times until the surface turns white. Then proceed with Step 1 of the Method.
2. Tripe from the second stomach of the beef looks like a honeycomb—hence, its name. It is the tenderest kind of tripe.
3. This soup looks milky white and tastes thick and substantial. Don't be dismayed by the unattractive appearance of the tripe before you cook it. It will have a delicious taste and a chewy texture in the soup. A traditional Korean belief is that this soup will cure tuberculosis. (The United States has its own tripe-soup tradition: a soup made with 100 pounds (45 kg) of donated tripe is often credited with putting heart into George Washington's starving troops at Valley Forge. The soup is now called Philadelphia Pepper Pot.)

Egg-Wrapped Skewers (*Kimchi Nu-reum Jeok*)

8 skewers

Ingredients:
6 eggs, lightly beaten with a pinch of salt
8 oz. (200 g) flank steak or thin-cut round steak
¼ bunch Chinese cabbage kimchi (about 8 oz. (200 g))
4–5 thin green onions
Seasoning Mixture (for beef)
   2 tablespoons soy sauce
   2 tablespoons minced green onion
   1 tablespoon minced garlic
   2 tablespoons prepared sesame seeds (see recipe, p. 11)
   1 tablespoon sesame oil
   Dash of pepper
4 tablespoons flour
Sesame oil
Vinegar-Soy Sauce (see recipe p. 11)

Method:
1. Lightly squeeze kimchi to remove excess liquid. Cut the kimchi and green onions into 2-inch (5 cm) lengths.
2. Cut the beef into pieces a little smaller than the kimchi, and mix the meat thoroughly with Seasoning Mixture.
3. Place the kimchi, green onions and beef (in that order) on bamboo skewers.
4. Dredge skewered ingredients with flour, shake off excess flour and then coat thoroughly with the beaten eggs.
5. Heat a little sesame oil in skillet and fry a skewer over medium heat, pouring a tablespoonful of the remaining eggs over the skewer. Don't let the egg brown. When meat is cooked, with chopsticks or spatula fold excess eggs toward skewer to wrap, and turn. Fry until light brown. Repeat the process with remaining skewers.
6. Arrange skewers on plate and serve with Vinegar-Soy Sauce.

Notes:
1. Strain beaten eggs if there is any foam.
2. Add ½ teaspoon sesame oil to the skillet if the egg starts to brown before the meat is cooked.
3. A recipe for Chinese cabbage kimchi can be found on page 52. Also, many Korean grocery stores sell home-made kimchi whose flavor is excellent.

Crab Meat Omelets (*Ke Al-ssam*)

12 omelets
Ingredients:
7 oz. (200 g) crab meat
3 eggs
Pinch of salt
2 tablespoons sesame oil
Vinegar-Soy Sauce (see recipe, p. 11)

Method:
1. Carefully remore crab meat from can.
2. Lightly beat eggs with a pinch of salt and pour through strainer to eliminate froth.
3. Heat a small skillet and coat it with a little of the sesame oil. Pour in 2 tablespoons of the beaten and strained egg, and tilt skillet to spread the egg thinly. Quickly reduce heat to medium-low to avoid burning the egg. Place a little of crab meat on the egg, and shape it into a line down the center of the omelet. Then quickly roll the egg around the crab meat, and lightly brown all sides.
4. Repeat Step 3 with the remaining egg and crab meat.
5. Arrange on serving dish and serve with Vinegar-Soy Sauce.

Fried Prawns (*Saewu Jeon*)

4 servings
Ingredients:
¾ lb. (300 g) prawns
2 eggs
3 tablespoons flour
Salt and pepper
3–4 tablespoons sesame oil
Vinegar-Soy Sauce (see recipe, p. 11)

Method:
1. Shell prawns, leaving on tails and the edge next to tail. Remove heads and veins. Make a cut along the inside curve and spread open. Wipe off with a paper towel and sprinkle with a little salt and pepper.
2. Beat eggs with a little salt. Be sure to beat lightly to prevent formation of air bubbles.
3. Dredge prawns with flour and shake off the excess. Coat with beaten eggs.
4. Heat the sesame oil in a skillet. Fry prawns until light brown, opening and lightly pressing the tails with a turner to form a good shape.
5. Serve with hot with Vinegar-Soy Sauce.

A Quartet of Korean Kebabs (*Sanjeok Kooi*)

4 servings

Beef and Green Onions

Ingredients:

1 lb. (400 g) beef (flank steak or thin-cut round steak)

6 thin green onions

Basting Sauce:
- 4 tablespoons soy sauce
- 2 tablespoons sugar

3 tablespoons minced green onion

1½ tablespoons minced garlic

1 tablespoon prepared sesame seeds (see recipe, p. 11)

2 tablespoons sesame oil

½ tablespoon *sul* or sherry

Dash of pepper

Method:

1. Slice beef into pieces the size of your little finger. Sprinkle a little of the Basting Sauce over beef (about 1 tablespoon or more to taste.)
2. Cut green onions the same length as the beef.
3. Alternately thread beef and green onions on bamboo skewers.
4. Grill outdoors or in oven broiler until cooked as desired. While cooking, baste with Basting Sauce. Serve hot.

Beef and Green Peppers

Ingredients:

¾ lb. (300 g) beef

20 sweet green chili peppers or 3–4 regular green peppers

Basting Sauce:
- 4 tablespoons soy sauce
- 2 tablespoons sugar

4 tablespoons minced green onion

1½ teaspoons minced garlic

2 teaspoons prepared sesame seeds (see recipe, p. 11)

1½ tablespoons sesame oil

1 teaspoon *sul* or sherry

Dash of pepper

Method:

Follow the directions for Beef and Green Onion Kebabs, substituting green peppers for the green onions. If using the sweet green chilis (and be sure they are sweet, not hot!), wash and stem them. If using regular green peppers, wash them, cut them open and remove seeds, then cut them into pieces the same size as the beef.

Beef and Chinese Mushrooms

Ingredients:

1 lb. (400 g) beef

5–6 fresh Chinese mushrooms

Basting Sauce:
- 4 tablespoons soy sauce
- 2 tablespoons sugar
- 4 tablespoons minced green onion

1½ tablespoons minced garlic

½ tablespoon *sul* or sherry

1 tablespoon prepared sesame seeds (see recipe, p. 11)

2 tablespoons sesame oil

Dash of pepper

Method:

Follow the directions for Beef and Green Onion Kebabs, substituting Chinese mushrooms for the green onions. Wash mushrooms, remove stems, and cut the same size as the beef. If dried Chinese mushrooms are the only ones available, soak them in warm water until very soft.

Beef Liver and Vegetables
Ingredients:

¾ lb. (300 g) beef liver (or chicken livers)
3 oz. (100 g) bamboo shoots
5 fresh Chinese mushrooms
3 thin green onions
3 oz. (100 g) carrot
Basting Sauce:
   5 tablespoons soy sauce

2½ tablespoons sugar
4 tablespoons minced green onion
2 teaspoons minced garlic
1 teaspoon minced fresh ginger
1 tablespoon prepared sesame seeds (see recipe, p. 11)
2 tablespoons sesame oil
Dash of pepper

Method:
1. Skin liver and cut into pieces the size of your little finger. Cut bamboo shoots, Chinese mushrooms, green onions, and carrot the same size as liver. Parboil carrot in salt water.
2. Alternately thread liver, green onions, mushrooms, carrot and bamboo shoots on skewers, and grill as above.

Seasoned Raw Beef (*Yuk Hoe*)

4 servings
Ingredients:
1 lb. (500 g) beef fillet
1 pear
1 egg yolk
Seasoning Mixture:
   4 tablespoons soy sauce
   2 tablespoons sugar
   2 tablespoons minced green onion
   1 teaspoon garlic juice
   2½ teaspoons prepared sesame seeds (see recipe, p. 11)
   2 tablespoons sesame oil
   Dash of pepper
3 tablespoons finely chopped pine nuts

Method:
1. Cut the beef into slender matchstick-sized pieces.
2. Combine beef and Seasoning Mixture; use a light hand when mixing to keep the shredded beef from forming clumps. Sprinkle with the pine nuts.
3. Place in mound on serving dish. Make a depression on top and slide the egg yolk into it.
4. Peel and core pear. Slice thinly, dip in salt water, then drain. Place on serving dish next to the beef.
5. The egg yolk is mixed into the meat before eating.

Note:
Pears are often combined with raw meat in Korean cooking. The Oriental pear is round and crisp, halfway between American apple and pear in taste and texture. This pear can occasionally found in the fall in supermarkets or oriental grocery stores. Ask for *bae* (Korean) or *nashi* (Japanese).

Braised Short Ribs *(Kalbi Jjim)*

4 servings

Ingredients:
2 lb. (800 g) short ribs, cut into 2-inch (5 cm) lengths
4 dried Chinese mushrooms
½ small pear
1 egg
1 tablespoon *sul* or sherry
Seasoning Mixture:
   4 tablespoons soy sauce
   2 tablespoons sugar
   4 tablespoons minced green onion
   2 teaspoons minced garlic
   1½ tablespoons prepared sesame seeds (see recipe, p. 11)
   2 tablespoons sesame oil
   Dash of pepper

Method:
1. Place mushrooms in warm water and let soak till soft. Then remove stems and cut into quarters. Reserve the water.
2. Slash the short ribs down to the bone in several places, being careful not to separate the meat from the bones.
3. Peel and grate the pear. Mix with the short ribs.
4. Combine ingredients for Seasoning Mixture in a bowl large enough to accommodate the short ribs. Add the ribs and mix thoroughly.
5. Place the ingredients from Step 4 and the quartered mushrooms in a saucepan. Bring to a boil over high heat, then reduce heat and simmer until meat becomes tender. At some point while meat is simmering, sprinkle with *sul* or sherry.
6. Also while meat is simmering, make Egg Decoration with the 1 egg (see recipe, p. 11). Cut into diamonds.
7. To serve, place short ribs and mushrooms on platter and garnish with Egg Decoration.

Notes:
1. Should liquid evaporate before meat is tender, add a little of the reserved mushroom water.
2. Save and refrigerate any extra mushroom water. It is very flavorful and can be used as part of the liquid in soups and gravies.

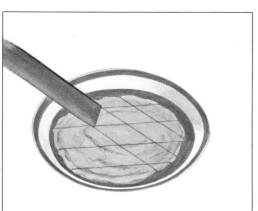

Broiled Chicken (*Dak-Dari Kooi*)

4 servings
Ingredients:
4 chicken thighs, boned
Seasoning Mixture:
   3 tablespoons soy sauce
   1½ tablespoons sugar
   3 tablespoons minced green onion
   1 teaspoon minced garlic
   ½ teaspoon minced fresh ginger
   2 teaspoons prepared sesame seeds (see recipe, p. 11)
   1½ tablespoons sesame oil
   Dash of pepper

Method:
1. Score chicken and steam 15–20 minutes.
2. Thoroughly combine ingredients of Seasoning Mixture.
3. When cooked, marinate chicken in Seasoning Mixture about one hour until well seasoned.
4. Broil chicken on heated grill, brushing with sauce, until golden brown and glossy.

Notes:
1. To bone a chicken thigh, put it on cutting board skin-side down. Make a cut down to and along thigh bone. Holding one end of bone, cut and scrape the meat away, and lift out the bone.
2. Marinating the chicken after steaming it produces an outstandingly delicious and unusual flavor.

Eggplant Sandwich (*Kaji Jijim*)

4 servings
Ingredients:
5 very small eggplants or 1 medium one
8 oz. (200 g) thinly sliced beef
4 tablespoons sesame oil
Seasoning Mixture:
   2 tablespoons soy sauce
   1 tablespoon sugar
   2 tablespoons chopped green onions
   1 teaspoon minced garlic
   2 teaspoons prepared sesame seeds (see recipe, p. 11)
   A little pepper
   1 tablespoon *sul* or sherry
   1 tablespoon sesame oil
Vinegar-Soy Sauce:
   3 tablespoons soy sauce
   1½ tablespoons vinegar
   ½ tablespoon lemon juice

Method:
1. Wash eggplants and remove stems. Cut into ⅜-inch (7 mm) slices, lengthwise for the small ones, crosswise for the medium one. Heat sesame oil in skillet and fry eggplant until golden brown.
2. Mix beef with mixture A and brown both sides on ungreased skillet.
3. Sandwich the beef between 2 slices of eggplant. Serve with Vinegar-Soy Sauce.

Note:
Oriental eggplants (3–5 inches (7.5–12.5 cm) long) or Italian eggplants (which are slightly larger) can be found in many supermarkets.

Cooked Tofu and Ground Meat (*Dubu Jjim*)

4 servings
Ingredients:
2 blocks tofu
5 oz. (150 g) ground beef
Mixture A:
    1½ tablespoons soy sauce
    ½ tablespoon minced green onion
    ⅔ teaspoon minced garlic
    1 tablespoon sesame oil
    Dash of pepper
Mixture B:
    2 tablespoons soy sauce
    2 teaspoons sugar
    3 tablespoons water
4 tablespoons sesame oil
1 green onion, thinly sliced
1 dried red pepper, finely shredded
½ tablespoon prepared sesame seeds (see recipe, p. 11)

Method:
1. Cut each block of tofu in half lengthwise, then crosswise into ⅜-inch (7 mm) slices. Spread a muslin dish towel or cheesecloth on a dry cutting board, wrap the tofu in it, and press lightly to remove excess water.
2. Thoroughly combine ground beef and Mixture A.
3. Heat skillet and pour in 4 tablespoons sesame oil. Fry both sides of sliced tofu until golden brown.
4. Spread seasoned beef on one side of fried tofu with a knife.
5. Place tofu in casserole meat-side up, and add Mixture B. Sprinkle with the sliced green onion, shredded red pepper, and the ground sesame seeds. Cook over medium heat until sauce is thickened. Serve hot in the casserole.

Note:
Heating the oil before adding tofu to the pan in Step 3 should keep the tofu from sticking to the bottom. If, despite your care, it does stick, pour in a little more sesame oil along the side of the pan.

Sunny Lettuce Wrap-Ups *(Sangchi Ssam)*

4 servings

Ingredients:

½ block tofu (about 4 oz.)
4 oz. (100 g) ground beef
Seasoning Mixture:
  2 tablespoons minced green onion
  1 teaspoon minced garlic
  ½ tablespoon sesame oil
  Dash of pepper

5 oz. (150 g) bean paste
1 tablespoon hot bean paste (see recipe, p. 11)
½ tablespoon sugar
1½ tablespoons sesame oil
1 tablespoon prepared sesame seeds (see recipe, p. 11)
1–2 heads of leaf lettuce
Cooked rice

Method:

1. Wrap tofu in cheesecloth or muslin dish towel and place on a tilted cutting board. Let it drain for 2 minutes.
2. Mix together ground beef and Seasoning Mixture.
3. Wash lettuce leaves and drain.
4. Heat a pan and brown the ground beef over medium heat.
5. Remove from stove. Add the tofu and the two kinds of bean paste, and mix thoroughly with the ground beef. Reheat over medium heat until the mixture thickens a little.
6. Stir in the sugar, and add the sesame oil little by little. Cook until it gets as thick as bean paste.
7. Place in a serving bowl and sprinkle on the sesame seeds. Serve with lettuce leaves and cooked rice.
8. To eat, place a spoonful of rice and some meat on a lettuce leaf and roll it up.

Fried Green Peppers (*Hokochu Jeon*)

4 servings

Ingredients:
16 small green peppers
5 medium sized green peppers
7 oz. (200 g) ground beef
Seasoning Mixture:
   2 tablespoons soy sauce
   2 tablespoons chopped green onion
   1 teaspoon minced garlic
   2 teaspoons prepared sesame seeds (see recipe, p. 11)
   2 tablespoons sesame oil
   A little pepper
3 tablespoons flour
2 eggs
A little salt
A little sesame oil
Vinegar-Soy Sauce (see recipe, p. 11)

Method:
1. Wash small green peppers. Remove stems, butterfly cut them and spread open, and remove seeds. Wash green peppers. Remove stems, cut crosswise into ¼-inch (5 mm) rings, and remove seeds.
2. Mix ground beef with Seasoning Mixture.
3. Stuff both kinds of peppers with the meat mixture.
4. Dredge the meat surfaces with flour, then coat the meat with eggs beaten with a little salt. Fry in sesame oil over low heat until cooked but not scorched.
5. Serve with Vinegar-Soy Sauce mixed with minced pine nuts.

Notes:
1. This dish may be served as an hors d'oeuvre.
2. Be sure the small green peppers are sweet and mild, not hot. If they are unavailable, increase the number of green peppers.

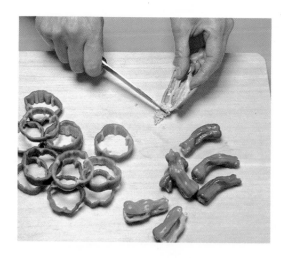

Mixed Vegetables (*Jap Chae*)

4 servings

Ingredients:

3 oz. (100 g) string beans
3 oz. (100 g) carrot
3 oz. (100 g) onion
3 oz. (100 g) bamboo shoots
1 rib of celery
5–6 dried Chinese mushrooms
5 cloud ears (see Ingredient, p. 11)
1½ oz. (50 g) Chinese vermicelli
7 oz. (200 g) thinly sliced beef
Seasoning Mixture:
  2 tablespoons soy sauce
  1 tablespoon sugar

3 tablespoons minced green onion
1 teaspoon minced garlic
1 tablespoon sesame oil
Dash of pepper
Sesame oil
2 eggs
2 tablespoons soy sauce
1 tablespoon sugar
A little salt
1½ tablespoons prepared sesame seeds (see recipe, p. 11)

Method:

1. Parboil string beans in salt water, submerge in cold water to preserve bright color, drain and shred. String celery stalk. Shred celery, carrot, bamboo shoot, and onion into 2-inch (5 cm) lengths. Soak dried Chinese mushrooms in water, remove stems and shred. Soak cloud ears in water, remove hard "eyes", and shred coarsely. Soak Chinese vermicelli in water, cut into several portions; let sit in colander to drain thoroughly.
2. Shred sliced beef, and combine with Chinese mushrooms and Seasoning Mixture.
3. Sauté shredded vegetables and vermicelli separately in sesame oil. When softened, sprinkle with a little salt to taste.
4. Quickly sauté beef, Chinese mushrooms and cloud ears over high heat.
5. Make Egg Decoration (see recipe, p. 11), and shred.
6. Save some of the Egg Decoration for garnishing the dish. Mix the rest with all the other cooked ingredients, and stir in the soy sauce, sugar, and sesame seeds. You may want to change the amount of soy sauce, depending on how much salt you used in Step 3.
7. Place in serving bowl and garnish with reserved Egg Decoration.

Note:

Though time consuming, it is important to sauté the vegetables separately to avoid overcooking or undercooking them and to preserve their individual character.

Potato Patties (*Kamja Buchim*)

4 servings

Ingredients:

4 potatoes
1 small green pepper
2 green onions
8 oz. (200 g) thinly sliced pork
Seasoning Mixture:
   2 tablespoons soy sauce
   2 tablespoons minced green onion
   1 teaspoon minced garlic
   2 teaspoons prepared sesame seeds (see recipe, p. 11)
   1 tablespoon sesame oil
   Dash of pepper
A little thinly shredded dried red pepper
½ teaspoon salt
A little sesame oil
Vinegar-Soy Sauce (see recipe, p. 11)

Method:

1. Pare potatoes and remove eyes. Let soak in cold water to eliminate harshness.
2. Remove stem and seeds from the small green pepper, and shred. Finely shred green onions.
3. Shred pork and marinate in Seasoning Mixture.
4. Quickly grate potatoes and add ½ teaspoon salt. Heat a skillet and pour in a little sesame oil. Drop in the grated potatoes, forming them into patties 2½ inches (6.5 cm) in diameter.
5. On top of each patty, place a portion of the pork, small green pepper, green onion and a little shredded red pepper. Fry both sides until golden brown.
6. Serve hot with Vinegar-Soy Sauce.

Notes:

1. In Step 4, immediately stir the salt into the grated potatoes to avoid discoloration.
2. For the most delicious flavor, be sure that the pork is well browned.
3. Finely shredded dried red pepper is very hot. Use sparingly.
4. Dried mung beans are used in another kind of Korean pancake. Soak overnight, then rub between the hands to remove the skins which will float to the top of the water. Grind in a blender with enough water to make a thick paste. Drop by tablespoons on to a greased skillet and brown both sides. Shredded pork, seasoned as above, or chopped kimchi can be added to the batter. Serve with Vinegar-Soy Sauce.

Cold Noodle (*Naeng Myeon*)

4 servings

Ingredients:

1 lb. (500 g) giant white radish
Mixture A:
  1 teaspoon powered red pepper
  1 tablespoon salt
  ½ teaspoon minced fresh ginger
  1 teaspoon minced garlic
  ¼ green onion, shredded
1 lb. (500 g) beef (brisket or bottom round)
½ clove of garlic, sliced
Mixture B:
  3 tablespoons minced green onion
  3 tablespoons light soy sauce
  1 tablespoon sesame oil
  1 tablespoon prepared sesame seeds (see

    recipe, p. 11)
  ½ teaspoon grated garlic
  Dash of pepper
2 cucumbers
Mixture C:
  1 tablespoon soy sauce
  1 tablespoon minced green onion
  1 teaspoon sesame oil
  A little finely shredded dried red pepper
2 eggs
1 pear
1 lb. (500 g) Korean or Chinese thin noodles
Finely shredded dried red pepper
Salt, light soy sauce, vinegar and mustard

Method:

1. Start preparing for the dish at least one day before serving. Cut giant white radish in half lengthwise and slice across very thinly. Combine with Mixture A. Let stand one day or more to make kimchi.

2. Bring 10 cups water to a boil and add beef, skim several times until scum is thoroughly removed, then add sliced garlic. Continue cooking over low heat about two hours. When a skewer or fork slides easily into the meat, remove from pot, slice thinly, and mix with Mixture B. Add a few drops of light soy sauce and salt to broth while hot. Strain and cool.

3. Cut cucumbers in half lengthwise and then across into thin slices. Combine with Mixture C.

4. Hardboil the eggs and shell them. Cut a slice off each end for balance in the final assembling, then cut them in half crosswise.

5. Peel and core the pear, and cut lengthwise into thin slices. Dip in salt water and drain.

6. Bring a large quantity of water to a boil, and add the noodles. Boil for 4 or 5 minutes, stirring with chopsticks or cooking spoon. Then rinse in cold water, rubbing noodles between your hands as shown in the picture.

7. Separate noodles into four portions and place them in large individual bowls, mounding them in a spiral shape. Place on top in the order given; kimchi, cucumbers, beef, pear and eggs. Garnish with a little shredded red pepper. Pour over a generous amount of chilled soup. Serve with soy sauce, vinegar, and mustard.

Note:
To simplify the preparation of this dish, you can make the soup as well as the kimchi a day ahead. You will also find the meat easier to slice and the fat easier to remove from the soup if you do so. Let the meat cool in the soup, but before refrigerating, remove it and wrap it tightly in foil.

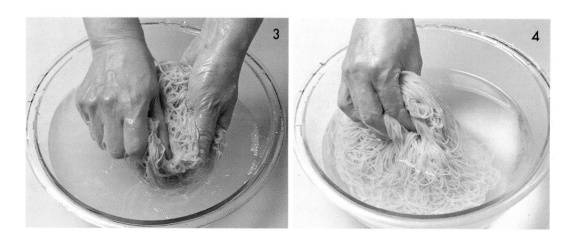

Garnished Rice (*Bibim Bap*)

4 servings

Ingredients:

5 cups cooked rice

8 oz. (200 g) flank steak or thin-cut round steak

Mixture A:
  2 tablespoons soy sauce
  1 tablespoon sesame oil
  2 teaspoons prepared sesame seeds
    (see recipe, p. 11)
  Dash of pepper
  1 teaspoon minced garlic
  2 tablespoons minced green onion

⅔ lb. (300 g) bracken, soaked in water and drained

1 tablespoon sesame oil

Mixture B:
  2½ tablespoons soy sauce
  ½ teaspoon sugar
  ½ teaspoon minced garlic
  1 tablespoon minced green onions

A little chili pepper

½ tablespoon prepared sesame seeds

3 cucumbers
  1½ teaspoons salt
  1 tablespoon sesame oil
  1 tablespoon minced green onions
  ½ tablespoon prepared sesame seeds

13 oz. (400 g) bean sprouts
  1½ cups water
  1 teaspoon salt

Mixture C:
  1½ tablespoons sesame oil
  1 tablespoon minced green onion
  1 tablespoon prepared sesame seeds

2 eggs
  Pinch of salt

Hot Bean Paste *Kochu Jang* (see recipe, p. 11)

Dried sea tangle: (also called kelp)
  (optional)

Method:
1. Slice beef as thinly as possible and mix with Mixture A. Panbroil, then shred the meat.
2. Remove the tough ends of the bracken and cut the remainder into 2-inch (5 cm) lengths. Mix with Mixture B and cook in 1 tablespoon sesame oil until flavors are well absorbed. Sprinkle with ½ tablespoon sesame seeds, and turn off heat.
3. Thinly slice cucumbers and sprinkle with 1½ teaspoons salt. Let sit until the slices become soft, then squeeze out moisture. Fry in 1 tablespoon sesame oil over high heat. After a moment, sprinkle with 1 tablespoon minced green onion, and continue to cook quickly over high heat until liquid has evaporated. Turn off heat and sprinkle with ½ tablespoon sesame seeds. Cool quickly.
4. Wash bean sprouts and put into 1½ cups water with 1 teaspoon salt. Bring to a boil and cook lightly. Drain and mix with Mixture C.
5. Make Egg Decoration, and shred. (see recipe, p. 11)
6. Put the cooked rice in a bowl, and sprinkle with a little sesame oil, if desired. Arrange the other ingredients over the rice, with the Egg Decoration and a little Kochujan on top. The diners help themselves, and mix everything together before eating. For additional flavor, dried sea tangle, fried crispy and crumbled, may be sprinkled over the dish.

Note:
Sprouts from mung beans are the ones most commonly found in supermarkets. In Oriental food stores you can often buy the larger sprouts from soy beans; use them in this dish if available. Remove the hairlike roots, and cook them for about 10 minutes until tender.

Chicken Salad (*Dak-Koki Muchim*)

4 servings

Ingredients:

1 lb. (500 g) chicken wings

10 green onions

Seasoning Mixture:

    3⅓ tablespoons soy sauce

    2 tablespoons minced green onion

    1 teaspoon minced garlic

    ½ teaspoon minced fresh ginger

    1 dried red pepper, shredded

    1 tablespoon prepared sesame seeds (see recipe, p. 11)

    2 tablespoons sesame oil

    Dash of pepper

Method:

1. Steam chicken wings about 10 minutes or until cooked. Cool, then with your fingers tear into thin strips.
2. Wash green onions and cut into 2-inch (5 cm) strips.
3. Combine chicken, green onions and Seasoning Mixture. Serve immediately.

Notes:

1. If you do not have a steamer, you can make one by placing an empty can with both ends removed in the center of a deep pot. Pour in boiling water to a level 1 inch (3 cm) below the top of the can. Place the chicken wings on a heat resistant plate and balance it on top of the can. Cover and maintain the boil. Have a kettle of boiling water ready if it becomes necessary to add more to the pot.
2. Don't let this dish sit too long before serving, or it gets soggy.

Fancy Fire Pot (*Sin-seon-lo*)

4 servings

Ingredients:

⅓ lb. (150 g) ground beef
Seasoning Mixture:
  1½ tablespoons soy sauce
  1½ tablespoons minced green onion
  ⅔ teaspoon minced garlic
  ½ tablespoon prepared sesame seeds (see recipe, p. 11)
  ⅔ tablespoon sesame seed oil
¼ lb. (100 g) lean beef
¼ lb. (100 g) beef liver
¼ lb. (100 g) white fish fillets
¼ lb. (100 g) *minari* or watercress

4–5 dried Chinese mushrooms
3 oz. (80 g) carrot
3 oz. (80 g) boiled bamboo shoots
½ onion
3 walnuts
12 ginkgo nuts
⅓ cup flour
5–6 eggs
4–5 tablespoons sesame oil
Soup Stock (beef) (see p. 14)
Salt and pepper

Method:

Please note that the following ingredients should all be cut in thin slices of the same length and width; carrot and bamboo shoots; beef, beef liver, and fish; thin omelets. The chives should be cut to the same length, and the mushrooms sliced on the diagonal as close to the same length as possible. You will have scraps left over from some of this cutting; these scraps will also be utilized in the final assembling of the dish.

1. Skin beef liver and slice thinly. Soak in cold water for 15 or 20 minutes, then drain.
2. Soak dried Chinese mushrooms in lukewarm water about 15 minutes. Drain, cut off and discard stems, and slice the caps on the diagonal.
3. Parboil carrot. Slice carrot and bamboo shoots. Remore the roots and leaf top of *minari* and cut it the same length.
4. Thinly slice fish fillets and beef.
5. Separate the yolks and whites of two of the eggs. Fry yolks and whites separately in thin omelets, then cut into rectangular pieces. Remember that all the ingredients in Steps 1–5 should be cut as uniformly as possible. Reserve the scraps.
6. Preparation of remaining ingredients: Thoroughly combine ground beef and Seasoning Mixture. With half of the ground beef, make tiny meatballs the size of marbles. With the other half, make larger meatballs the size of chestnuts. Shell walnuts; dip in hot water and remove the inner skin. Drain canned ginkgo nuts, or, if using fresh ones, shell them and remove inner skin. Cut onion in half, then into thin slices.
7. Preliminary cooking: Beat the remaining eggs with a pinch of salt. Sprinkle sliced beef, liver, and fish with a little salt and pepper. Dust with flour and coat with beaten eggs; do the same with the marble-sized meatballs and the *minari*. Heat the sesame oil in a skillet and sauté these ingredients in small batches.

Final assembling and table cooking:

Layer the sliced onion and Chestnut-sized meatballs at the bottom of a fire pot or cook-and-serve casserole or electric skillet. Spread over them the scraps from Steps 1–5. Then arrange on top as artistically as possible the evenly cut ingredients and the walnuts, ginkgo nuts, and the small meatballs. Pour in the soup stock and heat at the table. As the food becomes heated through, the guests serve themselves.

Note:

Fire pots are available at Oriental grocery stores and gourmet kitchen shops. If you are using one, cut the ingredients in Steps 1–5 to fit between the rim and the chimney.

Chestnut Sweets *(Bam Dasik)*

4 servings

Ingredients:
30 medium-sized chestnuts
2 tablespoons honey
3 tablespoons sugar
½ teaspoon cinnamon
1 tablespoon brandy
Pinch of salt

Method:
1. Boil chestnuts in large quantity of hot water until cooked. Remove the outer and inner shells.
2. Mash chestnuts, then strain through sieve to ensure a smooth texture.
3. Add remaining ingredients and mix well until thickened.
4. Stuff the mixture into small decorative molds, and unmold to serve.

Dried Persimmon Dessert *(Kotkam Seon)*

4 servings

Ingredients:
8 small dried persimmons
8–10 walnuts

Method:
1. Remove calyxes from dried persimmons. Cut lengthwise into them, but do not cut all the way through. Remove seeds.
2. Shell walnuts and remove the hard inside bits.
3. Generously stuff walnuts inside the persimmons. Close persimmons reforming them into their original shape.
4. Cut crosswise into ½-inch (1 cm) slices.

Note:
Select half-dried persimmons which are soft inside.

Chinese Cabbage Kimchi (*Baechu Kimchi*)

Kimchi is the Korean pickle. Made from several kinds of vegetables, it is served every day all year round.

When the weather starts to become bitterly cold, every Korean housewife makes various kinds of kimchi as one of her seasonal events. Kimchi keeps well even though its salt content is rather low. It is an important part of the Korean diet, especially during the long winter when fresh vegetables are scarce.

Ingredients:
8½ lb. (4 kg) Chinese cabbage
Salt water (8⅓ cups water and 1¼ cups salt)
3⅓ lb. (1.5 kg) giant white radish

10 stalks *minari* or watercress
2 cuttlefish
1 onion
4 tablespoons powdered red pepper
Mixture A:
    2½ tablespoons minced garlic
    1⅓ tablespoons minced fresh ginger
    2 green onions, miced
    ½ cup salted shrimp (see Ingredients, p. 11)
    2½ tablespoons salt
    2 tablespoons sugar
Mixture B:
    1 tablespoon giant white radish juice (see Note below)
    ⅘ cup chicken stock

½ tablespoon salt

Method:
1. Discard the outside leaves of Chinese cabbage and cut lengthwise into halves or quarters. Let soak in salted water for a whole day.
2. When Chinese cabbage has become wilted, place in colander to drain.
3. Shred giant white radish and mix with powdered red pepper. Let stand for 10 minutes.
4. Cut *minari* into 2-inch (5 cm) lengths. Slice onions thinly. Slice cuttlefish.
5. Thoroughly mix together the *minari*, onions, cuttlefish, Mixture A, and giant white radish.
6. Insert the mixture between leaves of drained Chinese cabbage. Reserve the juice from the mixture.
7. Tightly pack Chinese cabbage into a crock and pour in the juice from Step 6 and Mixture B.
8. Place a dish small enough to fit inside the crock on top of the Chinese cabbage in order to press it gently. Cover with plastic wrap. The kimchi will be ready to eat after a week at 44–46°F. (22°C.–25°C.). Then store in refrigerator.

Note:
To obtain white radish juice, grate the radish, then squeeze through a loosely woven cotton dish towel into a bowl.

Korean Hors d'Oeuvres (*Ku-jeol-pan*)

6 servings (*35 thin pancakes*)
Ingredients:

Pancakes:
  2 eggs
  ½ teaspoon salt
  2 cups flour
  2 cups water
5 oz. (150 g) beef, thinly sliced
Seasoning Mixture:
  1½ tablespoons minced green onion
  ½ teaspoon minced garlic
  1 teaspoon prepared sesame seeds. (see recipe, p. 11)
  1⅓ tablespoons soy sauce
  ½ tablespoon sugar

½ tablespoon sesame oil
Dash of pepper
1 large abalone (preferably fresh) or squid
5 oz. (150 g) canned crab meat
4 eggs
5 oz. (150 g) carrots
7 oz. (200 g) bamboo shoots
8 dried Chinese mushrooms
2 cucumbers
Minced green onion
Prepared sesame seeds (see recipe, p. 11)
Soy sauce, salt, sugar, sesame oil, and mustard

Method:
1. Beat eggs lightly with salt and water. Stir in flour, blend and strain. Heat oil and make thin pancakes 4 inches (10 cm) in diameter. Turn once, remvoing from pan before they brown. (You should have about 35 pancakes.)
2. Mix beef with Seasoning Mixture. Broil or panbroil until lightly browned. Shred.
3. Shred abalone. (If using a fresh abalone, first scrub it and boil briefly in the shell.)
4. Mix with a little minced green onion, soy sauce, sesame seeds, and sesame oil.
5. Shred carrots and sauté with a little sesame oil, minced green onion and salt to taste. Sprinkle with a few sesame seeds.
6. Drain bamboo shoots and shred. Sauté in the same way as carrots in Step 5.
7. Soak dried Chinese mushrooms in water until soft. Drain and shred. Sauté with a little sesame oil, minced green onion, soy sauce, and sugar to taste.
8. Pick over and flake crab meat.
9. Shred cucumbers and sprinkle with a little salt. When wilted, squeeze out moisture and quickly sauté over high heat, seasoning like carrots in step 5. Fan to cool quickly.
10. Make Egg Decoration (see recipe, p. 11). Shred.
11. Place the pancakes in the center of a round platter and surround with the 8 fillings. The guests spread a bit of mustard on a pancake, place a small amount of each of the fillings on top, roll it up and eat it with the fingers.

Note:
The mustard served with this dish should be very hot. To make it, put 3 tablespoons of powdered mustard in a bowl and gradually stir in 4 to 5 tablespoons cold water. Keep stirring until it forms a thin paste. Let it mellow for an hour or more before using.

Menu A
for
Family Dinner

Continued on pages 67–70

Kimchi,
Korean Hors d'Oeuvres,
Fried White Fish,
Braised Chicken with
Chestnuts and
Family Tray
—Brioled Cod,
Chrysanthemum Leaf
Salad,
Twice-Cooked Ground
Beef,
Beef Soup
and Plain Rice

Menu B
for *Sul*

Continued on pages 71–72

Grilled Meats

Menu C
for Family Party

Continued on pages 72–73

**Grilled Meats Wrap-Ups
and Pear Salad**

Cakes and Korean Tea

Continued on pages 74–76

Fried Date Cakes,
Fried Honey Cakes
and Korean *Yuja* Tea

Medicine Recipe

Continued on pages 76–77

Steamed Rice Pudding

Menu A for Family Dinner

Continued from page 56

Chinese Cabbage Kimchi
(*Baechu Kimchi*)

Korean Hors d'Oeuvres
(*Ku-jeol-pan*)

Fried White Fish
(*Saeng-seon Jeon*)

Braised Chicken with Chestnuts
(*Dak Jjim*)

Family Tray

Braised Chicken with Chestnuts (*Dak Jjim*)

4 servings

Ingredients:

2 lb. (1 kg) chicken, chopped, bones and all into
   1-inch (3 cm) pieces (see Note 1, below)
5 dried Chinese mushrooms
5 oz. (150 g) carrots
5 oz. (150 g) bamboo shoots
12 ginkgo nuts
6 chestnuts
Marinade:
   6 tablespoons soy sauce
   3 tablespoons sugar
   5 tablespoons minced green onion
   2 teaspoons minced garlic
   1 teaspoon minced fresh ginger
   2½ tablespoons sesame oil
   Dash of pepper
1⅓ tablespoons prepared sesame seeds (see
   recipe, p. 11)
1 egg for Egg Decoration (see recipe, p. 11)

Method:

1. Place chicken in marinade and let sit for about one hour.
2. Soak Chinese mushrooms in water. When soft, remove stem and cut in half. Reserve water in which mushrooms were soaked.
3. Roll-cut (see Note 2, below) the carrots and bamboo shoots into bite-size pieces. Shell and skin chestnuts.
4. Bring to a boil ½ cup of the reserved mushroom water. Add chicken, return to a rapid boil, then turn heat to low.

5. After chicken has simmered for 15 minutes, add carrots, bamboo shoots, mushrooms, chestnuts and gingko nuts. Simmer until tender. Occasionally flip ingredients to season evenly, holding pan by the edge with both hands; do not use a cooking spoon for this because the ingredients might break apart.
6. While chicken is cooking, make the Egg Decoration. Cut into diamonds.
7. When almost all the liquid in saucepan has evaporated, turn off heat. Add sesame seeds and mix. Transfer to serving dish, and garnish with Egg Decoration.

Notes:

1. To chop the chicken, first disjoint it, then with a heavy knife or cleaver whack sharply across the bones. An accommodating butcher will do this for you on his electrical equipment; give him a whole chicken, not a disjointed one.
2. To roll-cut, make a diagonal cut at one end of the vegetable, give it a quarter turn and cut again on the diagonal. Continue turning and cutting. Roll-cutting produces triangle-shaped pieces with 3 exposed surfaces to absorb the flavors of the braising liquid.
3. Canned ginkgo nuts need only be drained before cooking. Fresh ginkgoes should be shelled by pounding them with the dull edge of a knife. Then place in water over low heat, and remove inner skin by rubbing them with the back of a slotted spoon.

Family Tray

Broiled Cod (*Buk-eo Kooi*)

4 servings
Ingredients:
3 dried cod (*Buk-eo*)
Seasoning Mixture:
   3½ tablespoons soy sauce
   2 tablespoons sugar
   4 tablespoons chopped green onion
   2 teaspoons minced garlic
   1 teaspoon minced fresh ginger
   1½ tablespoons hot bean paste (see recipe, p. 11)
   1 tablespoon prepared sesame seeds (see recipe, p. 11)
   MSG (optional)
   A little finely shredded dried red pepper
   A little green onion, cut into 2-inch (5 cm) strips

Method:
1. Moisten dried cod with water. Pound on the back with a heavy knife handle or stick. Soak in water for 3–4 hours, then drain. Remove bone and fin. Cut into 2-inch (5 cm) pieces. Drain again and dip the pieces in Seasoning Mixture.
2. Broil over charcoal fire, basting with Seasoning Mixture 2–3 times.

Chrysanthemum Leaf Salad (*Ssukkat Muchim*)

4 servings
Ingredients:
1–2 bunches of chrysanthemum leaves
Salad Dressing:
   2 tablespoons soy sauce
   ½ tablespoon sugar
   1 tablespoon vinegar
   1 tablespoon chopped green onion
   A little grated garlic
   A little cayenne pepper
   ½ tablespoon prepared sesame seeds (see recipe, p. 11)
   1 tablespoon sesame oil

Method:
Cut off the tough ends of the chrysanthemum stems. Boil in salt water until tender. Drain and cut into 2-inch (5 cm) lengths. Combine with the dressing.

Note:
This is the edible or garland chrysanthemum found in Oriental grocery stores (*ssukkat* in Korean, *shungiku* in Japanese). The Western garden-varieties of chrysanthemum are inedible.

Twice-Cooked Ground Beef (*Yak Sanjeok*)

4 servings

Ingredients:

8 oz. (200 g) ground beef

Mixture A:
  2 tablespoons soy sauce
  1 tablespoon sugar
  2 tablespoons minced green onion
  1 teaspoon minced garlic
  2 teaspoons prepared sesame seeds (see recipe,
    p. 11)
  1 tablespoon sesame oil
  Dash of pepper

Mixture B:
  2 tablespoons soy sauce
  1 tablespoon sugar
  $2/3$ tablespoon *sul* or sherry
  $2/3$ tablespoon fresh ginger juice

2 tablespoons minced pine nuts

a little oil

4 sheets wax or parchment paper (4-inch (10 cm)
  squares)

Method:

1. Combine ground beef and Mixture A and mix well.
2. Grease the squares of paper. Place ¼ of the meat on each piece and spread, leaving a ½-inch (13 mm) margin on all sides. With knife make crisscrosses on surface.
3. Heat a heavy skillet and place in it one of the squares, meat side down. Immediately strip off the paper, and panbroil over medium heat. When the meat gives off some juice, turn and brown the other side. (Depending on the fat content of the meat, you may need to add some oil to the pan.)
4. Repeat Step 3 with the remaining portions. Let cool, and cut into 1-inch (3 cm) squares.
5. Place Mixture B in pan, add 2 tablespoons water, and bring to a boil. Add the meat and cook, tipping the pan occasionally, until the liquid has boiled down. Be careful not to burn.
6. Place on a serving dish, and sprinkle with pine nuts.

Fried White Fish
(*Saeng-seon Jeon*)

4 servings
Ingredients:
¾ lb. (300 g) white meat fish fillets
2 eggs
3 tablespoons flour
Salt and pepper
3–4 tablespoons sesame oil
Vinegar-Soy Sauce (see recipe, p. 11)

Method:
1. Slice fish into 1½-inch (4 cm) pieces, wipe off with paper towel and sprinkle with a little salt and pepper.
2. Break eggs in bowl. Add a little salt and beat lightly to avoid forming bubbles.
3. Dredge fish with flour and shake off the excess. Coat with beaten eggs.
4. Heat sesame oil in skillet and fry fish until light brown.
5. Serve hot on plate with Vinegar-Soy Sauce.

Note:
You can prepare small fish this way, also. Butterfly cut them and remove bones.

Chinese Cabbage Kimchi
(*Baechu Kimchi*)   See pages 52, 53, 82–87

Korean Hors d'Oeuvres
(*Ku-jeol-pan*)   See page 54

Beef Soup
(*Yangji-Meoi Komkuk*)   See page 14

Menu B for *Sul*

Continued from page 58

Grilled Meats
(*Bul Koki*)

Grilled Meats (*Bul-Koki*)

4 servings (each recipe)

TONGUE
Ingredients:

1 lb. (400 g) fresh beef tongue
Seasoning Mixture:
  3 tablespoons soy sauce
  1½ tablespoons sugar
  3 tablespoons minced green onion
  1½ teaspoons minced garlic
  1 teaspoon minced fresh ginger
  1 tablespoon prepared sesame seeds (see recipe,
    p. 11)
  A little pepper
1 tablespoon *sul* or sherry

Method:

1. Wrap the root of the tongue in a dish towel or cheesecloth and strike hard on cutting board to loosen the skin. Remove skin with knife, pulling the loose end with your free hand. Slice very thinly.
2. Mix sliced tongue and Seasoning Mixture. Sprinkle with the *sul* and mix again.
3. Grill over charcoal or panbroil until thoroughly cooked.

Notes:

1. The tongue may become tough if allowed to marinate in the Seasoning Mixture for a long time, so mix the two just before cooking.
2. The tongue and the meats in the following recipes are traditionally cooked at the table on a special grill over charcoal. You can achieve the same effect with an electric skillet. Pour in a little sesame oil if the meat sticks. The diners help themselves to the slices of meat as they become cooked.

SIRLOIN (BEEF)
Ingredients:

1 lb. (5oo g) thinly sliced sirloin
Seasoning Mixture:
  4 tablespoons soy sauce
  2 tablespoons sugar
  4 tablespoons minced green onion
  2 teaspoons minced garlic
  1⅓ tablespoons prepared sesame seeds (see recipe, p. 11)
  2 tablespoons sesame oil
  Dash of pepper
2 tablespoons *sul* or sherry

Method:

1. Thoroughly mix sliced sirloin with Seasoning Mixture, and sprinkle with the *sul* for flavor.
2. Grill or panbroil soon after combining the meat and seasonings to keep the meat tender.

CHICKEN FILLETS
Ingredients:

1 lb. (500 g) chicken fillets
Seasoning Mixture:
  4 tablespoons soy sauce
  2 tablespoons sugar
  3 tablespoons minced green onion
  1½ teaspoons minced garlic
  1 teaspoon minced fresh ginger
  1 tablespoon prepared sesame seeds (see recipe,
    p. 11)
  2 tablespoons sesame oil
  a dash of pepper
1 tablespoon *sul* or sherry

Method:

1. Remove the tendon of chicken fillet. Cut crosswide into two pieces, then butterfly cut each piece and spread it open.
2. Thoroughly mix sliced fillets and Seasoning Mixture. Sprinkle with 1 tablespoon *sul* and mix again.
3. Grill or panbroil.

Note:

If fillets are not available, chicken breasts, boned and skinned, can be substituted. Cut into pieces 2 by 3 inches (5 × 7.5 cm).

SPAREIBS
Ingredients:

2 lb. (1 kg) spareribs
Seasoning Mixture:
  4½ tablespoons soy sauce
  2½ tablespoons sugar
  4 tablespoons minced green onion
  2½ teaspoons minced garlic
  1½ teaspoons minced fresh ginger
  ½ tablespoon hto bean paste (see recipe, p. 11)
  1½ tablespoons prepared sesame seeds (see recipe, p. 11)
  2 tablespoons sesame oil
  Dash of pepper
1 tablespoon *sul* or sherry

Method:

1. Separate the spareribs. Slash meat on both sides of the bone. Also, slash across the top if the ribs are meaty.
2. Thoroughly mix spareribs and Seasoning Mixture. Sprinkle with the *sul* and let mixture soak into slashes.
3. Grill or panbroil until thoroughly cooked.

Note:

Koreans observe a friendly and informal custom with this dish. Without waiting for the ribs to be cooked through, they nibble at the browned edges of the meat, then put the ribs back on the grill to finish cooking.

BEEF HEART

Ingredients:

1 lb. (400 g) thinly sliced beef heart

Seasoning Mixture:
   3 tablespoons soy sauce
   1½ tablespoons sugar
   3 tablespoons minced green onion
   1½ teaspoons minced garlic
   1 teaspoon minced fresh ginger
   1 tablespoon prepared sesame seeds (see recipe, p. 11)
   1½ tablespoons sesame oil
   Dash of pepper
1 tablespoon *sul* or sherry

Method:

1. Cut heart into halves in lengthwise and wash clean. Cut the half into two or four portions and skin. Slice thinly.
2. Just before cooking, mix meat and Seasoning Mixture. Sprinkle with the *sul* and mix again.

Menu C for Family Party

Continued from page 60

Grilled Meats Wrap-Ups
(*Bul-Koki Ssam*)

Pear Salad
(*Bae Saeng-Chae*)

Grilled Meats Wrap-Ups

(*Bul-Koki Ssam*)   See pages 34, 71

Pear Salad

(*Bae Saeng-Chae*)

4 servings

Ingredients:
¼ lb. (100 g) carrot
1 cucumber
3 leaves cabbage or lettuce
1 rib of celery
½ pear
5–6 green onions
1 tablespoon prepared sesame seeds (see recipe,
  p. 11)

Dressing:
  ½ tablespoon vinegar
  1½ tablespoons lemon juice
  ⅔ tablespoon sugar
  1 tablespoon sesame oil
  ½ teaspoon salt

Method:
Cut the first six ingredients into fine strips 1¾-inch (4 cm) long. Combine with sesame seeds and Dressing.

Cakes and Korean Tea

Continued from page 62

Fried Date Cakes
(*Mandu-Kwa*)

Fried Honey Cakes
(*Yak-Kwa*)

Korean *Yuja* Tea
(*Yuja Cha*)

Fried Date Cakes
(*Mandu-Kwa*)

70 cookies
Ingredients:
2½ cups flour
7 tablespoons sesame oil
Mixture A:
  3 tablespoons water
  3 tablespoons *sul* or sherry
  1 tablespoon sugar
  Pinch of salt
½ cup dried dates
¼ cup minced pine nuts
Mixture B:
  1½ cups honey
  ½ teaspoon cinnamon
  ½ tablespoon fresh ginger juice
  Grated rind of ½ *yuja* or lemon
Oil for deep-frying

Method:
1. Put dates and steam. While hot, mash and strain. Add minced pine nuts and a little cinnamon to taste. Mix well and make tiny balls the size of green peas.
2. Sift flour into bowl. Add sesame oil and combine well as for pie crust. Little by little add Mixture A to the flour, mixing thoroughly until all the flour is incorporated into the dough.
4. Pinch off pieces of the dough and roll into 1-inch (3 cm) balls. Depress the center with a thimble or your thumb and place a date ball from Step 1 in the depression. Bring opposite edges together, making pleats on the edge to close tightly. Pierce the shell to let out air while frying.

5. Heat a large quantity of oil to a high temperature and reduce heat to 210°F. (100°C.). Deep-fry the the cookies until well cooked.
6. Soak the hot cookies in Mixture B. After about 4 hours, drain well and serve.

Fried Honey Cakes
(*Yak-Kwa*)

40 cakes
Ingredients:
2½ cups flour
Mixture A:
  7 tablespoons sesame oil
  3 tablespoons water
  3 tablespoons *sul* or sherry
  1 tablespoon sugar
  Pinch of salt
Mixture B:
  2 cups honey
  ½ teaspoon cinnamon
  Grated rind of ½ *yuja* or lemon
  2 teaspoons fresh ginger juice
  Oil for deep-frying

Method:
1. Make dough in the same way as in Steps 2 and 3 of Fried Date Cookies. Shape in cookie molds, or press the dough into an oblong shape ¼ inch (6 mm) thick and cut into 2-inch (5 cm) squares.
2. Heat a large quantity of oil to a high temperature, then reduce heat to 210°F. (100°C.). Deep-fry cookies slowly until the layers can be seen and the surface becomes an even light brown.
3. Soak fried cookies in Mixture B until well sweetened. Drain and serve.

74

Korean *Yuja* Tea (*Yuja Cha*)

Ingredients:
2 *yuja* citrons
1 cup sugar
2 tablespoons pine nuts

Method:
Wash and slice *yuja* in thin pieces. Put sliced *yuja* in a pot and sprinkle sugar. Repeat process. Let stand overnight. Put a slice of *yuja* and 1 teaspoon *yuja* liquid in a tea cup. Add hot water and sprinkle with pine nuts on top.

Medicine Recipe

Continued from page 64

Steamed Rice Pudding
(*Yak-Sik*)

Steamed Rice Pudding (*Yak-Sik*)

10 servings
Ingredients:
3⅓ cups glutinous rice
1 lb. (500 g) chestnuts
5 oz. (150 g) dates
Seasoning Mixture:
   3 tablespoons soy sauce
   ½ cup dark brown sugar
   1½ cups sugar
3½ tablespoons sesame oil
1 teaspoon cinnamon
5 oz. (150 g) raisins
¼ cup honey
2 tablespoons pine nuts

Method:
1. Wash glutinous rice and soak in water for overnight.
2. Shell chestnuts and cut into halves.
3. Wash and pit dates, and cut into 2 or 3 pieces.
4. Drain rice, and place in a' steamer basket. Make a hole in the center of rice. Steam over high heat about 30 minutes until cooked. Sprinkle with ½ cup water during steaming.
5. Transfer rice to a large bowl. Add Seasoning Mixture to the hot rice and mix well. Add

sesame oil and cinnamon, and mix thoroughly once more.

6. Gently stir in the raisins, dates and chestnuts.

7. Place the bowl of rice pudding in the steamer and steam about 5 hours until chestnuts are cooked. Add more boiling water as needed. Sprinkle with honey and mix while steaming. Sprinkle with pine nuts before turning off heat.

Notes:

1. Use a wooden spoon to fold in the ingredients in Step 5.

2. This pudding is called *Yak-Sik* in Korean, which means "medicine food." *Yak* is often used in the name for honey-flavored sweets, because honey is good for the health and is sometimes used medicinally by Koreans.

3. The hot steamed rice pudding can be packed into a round cake pan, unmolded and cut into pieces before placing on serving dish.

Dried Beef (*Yuk-Po*)

Ingredients:
1 lb. (500 g) beef (round roast)
Seasoning Mixture:
    4 tablespoons soy sauce
    1½ tablespoons honey
    1 tablespoon *sul* or sherry
    Dash of pepper
Pine nuts

Methods:
1. Cut beef into slices as large as possible, but only ⅛-inch (3 mm) thick.
2. Marinate sliced beef in Seasoning Mixture for 20 minutes.
3. Spread marinated beef on flat basket or wire rack. Dry in the sun, turning it from time to time. Let stand until completely dried. (A, B)
4. Broil, then cut into bite-sized pieces. Sprinkle with pine nuts.

Pickled Spring Garlic (*Maneul Jang-ajji*)

Ingredients:
30 whole heads of young garlic
2 cups vinegar
2 cups soy sauce
⅔ cup sugar

Method:
1. Select young garlic heads with no sprouts. Remove roots and stems, wash, and peel off the outside skin. Place in bowl or jar and pour in the vinegar. Allow to stand for 4 or 5 days, turning the heads occasionally.
2. When the garlic has lost its harsh taste, drain off the vinegar.
3. Boil the soy sauce with the sugar for a few minutes, and let cool. Pour the cooled soy sauce over the garlic, seal the jar and let it sit for at least 2 months.
4. To serve, slice across the heads.

Notes:
1. Pickled garlic can be made only in early spring when soft, young heads are available.
2. It is very important to let the boiled soy sauce cool before combining with the garlic. Cooling prevents the garlic from going bad.
3. Garlic prepared this way loses all of its characteristic strong odor.

Korean Steamed Egg Custard (*Al Jjike*)

4 servings

Ingredients:

5 eggs

3 oz. (100 g) ground beef

Seasoning Mixture:

    ½ tablespoon soy sauce

    1 tablespoon minced green onion

    ⅓ teaspoon minced onion

    1 teaspoon prepared sesame seeds (see recipe,
      p. 11)

    1 teaspoon sesame oil

    Dash of pepper

6 tablespoons water

1½ tablespoon salted shrimp

2 tablespoon chopped green onion

Dash of powdered red pepper

Method:

1. In bowl combine ingredients of Seasoning Mixture and stir well.
2. Add ground beef and mix well. Make 20 very small meatballs the size of marbles.
3. Beat eggs. Add the water and salted shrimp and mix well but gently to avoid air bubbles.
4. Strain egg mixture to ensure a smooth custard.
5. Place 5 meatballs in each of 4 individual bowls and pour egg mixture over meatballs.
6. Bring 1½-inches (3.5 cm) water to a hard boil in a steam cooker.
7. Without covering bowls, place them in hot steam cooker. Wrap a dish towel around the steamer lid and place on steamer. Be sure the ends of the towel rest securely on top of the lid. The towel prevents water from dropping into custard.
8. Steam over high heat until just the surface of custard is cooked. Reduce heat immediately and sprinkle with chopped green onion, and powdered red pepper.
9. Steam about 20 more minutes. When soup comes out clear, custard is ready to serve.

Note:

This egg custard is a non-dessert dish. It would be served as one of the dishes in the main part of a Korean meal. Koreans also eat the custard at breakfast. Another idea: serve it in place of soup at the beginning of a Western-style meal.

Pickled Giant White Radish (*Kkak-du-ki*)

Ingredients:

2 lb. (1 kg) giant white radish
2 tablespoons powdered red pepper
1 apple
3 tablespoons salted shrimp (see Ingredients,
  p. 11)
½ tablespoon minced garlic
¼ tablespoon minced fresh ginger
2 green onions, shredded
2 tablespoons sugar, heated until dissolved
2½ tablespoons salt

Method:

1. Pare and cut giant white radish into ¾-inch
   (2 cm) cubes. Sprinkle with 2 tablespoons salt
   and let stand 1 hour. When softened, drain
   and sprinkle with powdered red pepper. Grate
   apple.
2. Put the ingredients from Step 1 into bowl. Add
   salted shrimp, garlic, ginger, green onion, ½
   tablespoon salt, and dissolved sugar. Mix well
   and pack in a crock or enameled container.
   Place a smaller lid or dish on top of pickles

before covering with plastic wrap or the lid
of the crock. Let stand 4 days at 50°F. (10°C.).

Eggplant Kimchi (*Kaji Kimchi*)

Ingredients:
10 small Oriental eggplants
Salt water (¾ cup water and 1 tablespoon salt)
Mixture A:
  1 teaspoon minced garlic
  ½ teaspoon minced fresh ginger
  3 tablespoons minced green onion
  1 tablespoon powdered red pepper
  1 tablespoon juice of salted shrimp (see
    Ingredients, p. 11)
  A little finely shredded dried red pepper
  ½ teaspoon salt
  1 teaspoon sugar
Mixture B:
  2½ tablespoons vinegar
  ¼ cup soy sauce
  2½ tablespoons sugar

Method:
1. Stem eggplants and make a deep lengthwise
   slash with knife point (on each). Soak in salt
   water about one hour. When softened,
   squeeze out, but do not wash.

2. Combine Mixture A and insert into all the
   slashes. Pack eggplants in a crock or enameled
   container and place two saucers on top.
   Combine Mixture B and pour over eggplants.
   Cover and let stand one night.
3. Cut eggplants lengthwise in half and serve.

Note:
If you want to keep this dish for a fairly long
time, omit vinegar in Mixture B.

Wrapped Kimchi (*Bossam Kimchi*)

This is the king of Kimchi with Chinese cabbage stuffed with fish and shellfish.

Ingredients:
8–9 lb. (4 kg) Chinese cabbage
Salt water (8½ cups water and 1½ cups salt)
1 lb. (500 g) giant white radish
½ pear
4–5 chestnuts, shelled
4–5 dates, pitted
1 bundle of *minari* or watercress
1 onion
1 boiled octopus leg or 1 squid
7 oz. (200 g) shrimp
1 abalone
5 oz. (150 g) oysters
3 tablespoons minced garlic
1½ tablespoons minced fresh ginger
3 green onions, minced
3 tablespoons powdered red pepper
A little shredded dried red pepper
½ cup salted shrimp (see Ingredients, p. 11)
3 tablespoons pine nuts
3½ tablespoons salt
2 tablespoons sugar
¾ cup juice of grated giant white radish
¾ cup broth (chicken stock)

Method:
1. Cut Chinese cabbage lengthwise into halves and soak in salt water for one day. When wilted, place in a colander cut side down to drain.
2. Cut giant white radish, onion, shelled chestnuts and pitted dates into thin strips. Cut the peeled pear in quarters, remove core and slice. Cut *minari* into 2-inch (5 cm) lengths.
3. Slice octopus leg thinly or skin the squid, remove intestines and slice. Shell shrimp and remove black vein; mash by chopping with the back of a heavy knife. Remove abalone meat from shell, wash well, and slice thinly. Wash oysters in a little salty water briefly and drain.
4. Put all the ingredients prepared in Steps 2 and 3 into bowl. Add in this order: garlic, fresh ginger, and green onion (all minced), powdered red pepper, shredded red pepper, salted shrimp, 3 tablespoons salt and sugar. Mix well.
5. Discard hard core from Chinese cabbage prepared in Step 1. Cut 2 inches (5 cm) off the white stem end of the leaves, then cut the stem end lengthwise in half.

6. Arrange 4–5 Chinese cabbage leaves like petals around the bottom and sides of a 2–3 cup bowl. Fill in the center with the stem ends, standing them upright and placing them in concentric circles. Insert the mixture from Step 4 between stems. Put about 10 pine nuts on top, and wrap the leaves around the filling. Remove from the bowl very carefully, and place in an earthenware crock or enameled container.
7. Repeat Step 6 with the remaining ingredients. Pack the cabbage rolls tightly into the crock.
8. There will be liquid left over from the Step 4 mixture. To this liquid, add ¾ cup of juice from the grated giant white radish, the stock and ½ tablespoon salt. Mix well and pour into the crock. Place a dish smaller than the crock on top of the Chinese cabbage to press it down. Cover and let stand 1 week at 45°F. (7–8°C.).
9. When serving, cut leaves open at the top.

84

Cucumber Kimchi
(*Oi Kimchi*)

Ingredients:
2 lb. (1 kg) cucumbers
7 oz. (200 g) giant white radish
2 green onions, shredded
2 teaspoons minced garlic
½ tablespoon minced fresh ginger
1 teaspoon powdered red pepper, if desired
¾ cup juice of grated giant white radish (see Note, p. 53)
4½ tablespoons salt
1 tablespoon sugar

Method:
1. Sprinkle cucumbers with 3 tablespoons salt and rub. When softened, wash and cut off both ends. Cut in half crosswise and make a deep lengthwise slash with the point of a knife on each half.
2. Shred giant white radish and sprinkle with powdered pepper. Mix green onion, garlic, giner, and 1 tablespoon salt well. Insert the mixture into slashes and pack in a crock or enameled container.
3. Mix giant white radish juice, 2½ cups water and ½ tablespoon salt together and pour over cucumbers. Place a weight on the cucumbers heavy enough to immerse them in the brine and cover the crock with plastic wrap or its own lid. Let stand 2 days at 72°F. (22°C.).

Note:
Do not use cucumbers with waxed skins. Unwaxed cucumbers are available at farmers' markets, health food stores, and co-ops. If using very small pickling cucumbers, cut off the ends but do not cut in half in Step 1.

Cabbage Kimchi
(*Yang-Baechu Tong-Kimchi*)

Ingredients:
4 lb. (2 kg) cabbage (about 2 heads)
Salt water (4–5 cups water and ½ cup salt)
1¾ lb. (700 g) giant white radish
1 bunch of green onions, green parts only
3–4 tablespoons powdered red pepper
1½ teaspoons minced fresh ginger
1 green onion, shredded
3–4 tablespoons salted shrimp (see Ingredients, p. 11)
1½ tablespoons sugar, heated until dissolved
¾ cup juice of grated giant white radish (see Note, p. 53)
Salt

Method:
1. Cut cabbage lengthwise into quarters. Soak in salt water 2–3 hours until wilted, then drain.
2. Cut giant white radish into thin strips and sprinkle with cayenne pepper. Cut the bunch of green onions into 2-inch (5 cm) lengths.
3. In bowl mix garlic, ginger, shredded green onion, salted shrimp, dissloved sugar, 1 tablespoon salt and ingredients from Step 2.
4. Insert the mixture from Step 3 between the leaves of the drained cabbage. Pack the cabbage into a crock or enameled container.
5. Using the bowl from the Step 3 mixture, pour in the radish juice and 1 teaspoon salt. Mix well and pour over the cabbage.
6. Place a smaller dish on top of cabbage and let stand 3 days at 60°F. (16°C.)

Note:
In some Korean and Japanese grocery stores you can find a pungent green onion called *buchu* (Korean) or *nira* (Japanese). Use this in place of the Chives.

Pickled Onion and Chinese Cabbage (*Okpa Kimchi*)

Ingredients:
1 onion
2 lb. (1 kg) Chinese cabbage
4 tablespoons salt
5–6 chili peppers, seeds removed
2 cloves garlic
1-inch (3 cm) piece fresh ginger
2 green onions, cut into strips
½ tablespoon sugar
¾ cup juice of grated giant white radish (see Note, p. 53)

Method:
1. Peel onion and slice thinly. Separate rings.
2. Cut Chinese cabbage into 1½-inch (4 cm) slices. Wash and sprinkle with 3 tablespoons salt.
3. When Chinese cabbage has become soft, rinse and drain.
4. Thoroughly grind garlic, ginger, and seeded chili peppers in a mortar.
5. Add giant white radish juice and grind again. Add green onion, Chinese cabbage, onion, sugar and about 1 tablespoon salt.
6. Transfer all the ingredients into a crock and place a smaller lid on top. Cover and let stand 2 days.

Note:
In Step 3, you can use a blender instead of a mortar. Gradually add the giant white radish juice as needed to blend.

Rice with Kimchi (*Kimchi Bap*)

4 servings

Ingredients:

2½ cups rice

¼ bunch Chinese cabbage kimchi
(about 7 oz. (200 g))

7 oz. (200 g) beef, thinly sliced

Seasoning Mixture:

   3 tablespoons soy sauce

   1 tablespoon sesame oil

   1 tablespoon prepared sesame seeds (see recipe,
     p. 11)

   2 tablespoons minced green onion

   1 teaspoon minced garlic

   Dash of pepper

3⅓ cups or 3½ cups water

2 tablespoons sesame oil

2 eggs

A pinch of salt

Method:

1. Shred kimchi without rinsing.
2. Shred beef and marinate in Seasoning Mixture.
3. Sauté rice in sesame oil until translucent.
4. In deep pan place first ⅓ of the rice, then ⅓ of the meat, and finally ⅓ of the kimchi. Repeat the process two more times and add 3⅓ cups water. Cook as for rice.
5. While cooking rice, make Egg Decoration, and shred. (see recipe, p. 11)
6. Serve rice with shredded Egg Decoration on top.

Note:

The flavor of this dish depends a great deal on the quality of the kimchi.

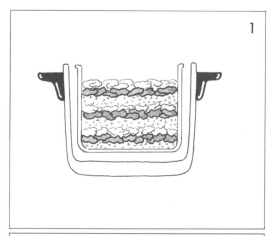

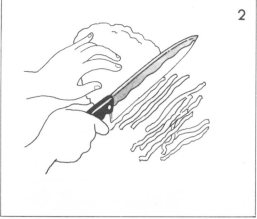

Ginger Candy

(*Saeng Pyeon*)

30 candies

Ingredients:

5 oz. (150 g) fresh ginger
5 oz. (150 g) sugar
½ teaspoon cinnamon
½ cup minced pine nuts

Method:

1. Pare ginger and boil for 3–4 minutes in water to remove its sharp taste. Drain and mince. You should have about ¾ cup.
2. Place ginger, sugar, and cinnamon in a heavy pan. Cook over low heat, stirring quickly.
3. When the mixture becomes very sticky and all the liquid has evaporated, remove pan from heat. Let it cool a little, then make ginger-shaped candies and ball candies. Coat candies with minced pine nuts.

Pine Nut Candy
(*Jat Kang-jeong*)

24 candies
Ingredients:
2½ cups pine nuts
A little angelica
2 oz. (60 g) maltose candies
⅔ cup sugar

Method:
1. In a heavy pan mix maltose candies and ½ cup sugar. Simmer over low heat, stirring occasionally. Check the thickness by dripping small amount of syrup into cold water.
2. When syrup forms a thread (at about 230°F, (110°C), if using a candy thermometer), add pine nuts, and mix quickly.
3. Place on a cutting board sprinkled with sugar. Quickly roll to a ⅓-inch (1 cm) thickness and cut into ½ × 1 inch (1.5 cm × 3 cm) bars. Garnish with angelica.

Note:
If maltose candies are unavailable, sugar syrup will be substituted.
Sugar Syrup:
⅔ cup sugar
½ cup water
2½ tablespoons white corn syrup
⅛ teaspoon salt
⅓ teaspoon cider vinegar
Put sugar syrup ingredients in a heavy pan and stir until sugar is dissolved. Bring to a boil, cover and cook for about 3 minutes until the steam has washed down the sides of the pan. Uncover and cook without stirring until almost to the hard-crack stage, 290°F. (143°C.). (If not using a candy thermometer, drop a small amount of syrup into cold water. The syrup will separate into hard threads.)

Sesame Candy
(*Kkae Kang-jeong*)

35 candies
Ingredients:
1 cup sesame seeds
3–4 dried dates
2–3 dried stone mushrooms
2 oz. (60 g) maltose candies
1 cup sugar
⅓ teaspoon cinnamon
1 tablespoon ginger juice

Method:
1. Heat sesame seeds until they begin to jump in pan; use low heat to avoid burning. Pit and shred dates. Soak stone mushrooms in hot water and shred.
2. Simmer maltose candies and half quantity of the sugar as in Step 2 "Pine Nut Candy."
3. When syrup forms a thread, add toasted sesame seeds, cinnamon and ginger juice. Mix together quickly.
4. Place on a cutting board sprinkled with sugar. Distribute dates and stone mushrooms over it. Quickly roll to a ⅛-inch (2 mm) thickness, and cut into 1-inch (3 cm) diamonds. When cool, store in a tightly sealed container.

Notes:
1. If stone mushrooms are not available, use extra dates.
2. To obtain ginger juice, crush thin slices in a garlic press; be sure to scrub the press clean of all traces of garlic. Another method is to grate fresh ginger and squeeze it through several layers of cheesecloth.
3. A variation of this recipe produces pinwheel candies. Use ½ cup black sesame seeds and ½ cup white ones. Omit dates and stone mushrooms. Cook syrup in 2 pans and add the black sesame seeds to one and the white to the other. Roll out separately, then place one on top of the other. Roll up together jelly-roll and cut into slices.

Vegetables

Fresh ginger roots

Garlic

Minari

Young ginger or ginger shoots

Red peppers

Yuja citron

Water chestnuts

Brockens

Ginkgo nuts

Fresh Chinese mushrooms

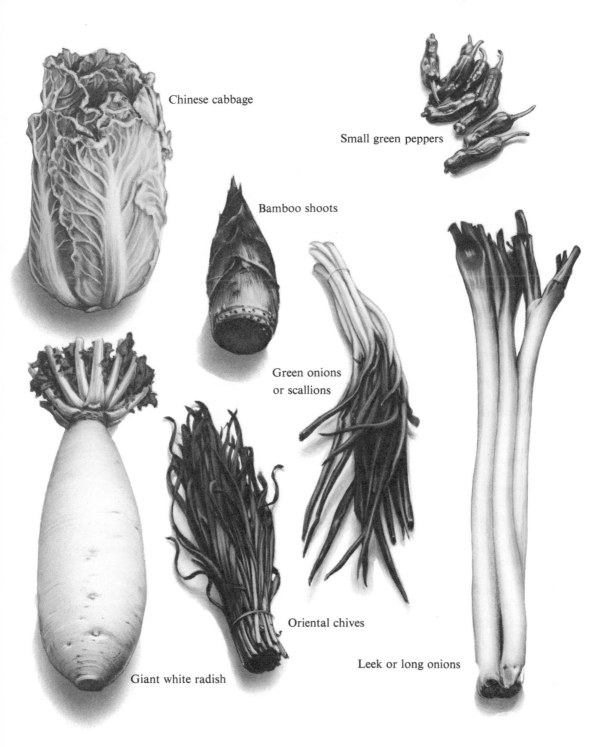

Chinese cabbage

Small green peppers

Bamboo shoots

Green onions
or scallions

Oriental chives

Leek or long onions

Giant white radish

93

Korean Table Settings

I. *Ban Sang*

At an informal meal, rice is the central dish of the main course. It is accompanied by various numbers of other dishes. Three, five or seven are the most usual combinations of dishes in home-style cooking. In court cooking, a tradition which a few distinguished families still follow, 9 or 12 dishes accompany the rice. "*Cheop*" means a kind of tableware with a lid, so seven "*Cheop*" indicates a combination of seven dishes with the rice. (Kimchi, soup or a casserole dish should not be included in this number.)

In former days Confucian beliefs dictated the order in which people were served. First came the elder members of the family and then the children. The last to eat were the women, which was not only the Confucian thing to do but also practical because it was the women who had to clean up the leftovers. However, the eating habits of Koreans have changed greatly, and these days they enjoy chatting over dishes on a round table surrounded by all the members of the family.

The most common combination of seven dishes is as follows:

1) *Jeon-yu-eo:* Fish or shell fish, in some cases meat, coated with egg and fried in a skillet.
2) *Ku-eun Chan:* Beef, pork, chicken, or fish, in some cases dried sea weed, broiled on a grill.
3) *Jochi:* Soup containing bean curd, vegetables, meat, fish, or eggs, and seasoned with bean paste, hot bean paste, or soy sauce.
4) *Mareun Chan:* Dried *Myeong-tae-eo* roe, cod fish and some other fish, fried eggs, *Eo-Po, Yuk-Po*, abalone or clams are also included in this category.
5) *Jeot-kal:* Salted oysters, shell fish, crab meat, cod roe, or *Myeong-tae-eo*.
6) Vegetables*:* A platter of several kinds of vegetables like bean sprouts, giant white radish, pumpkin, cucumbers, eggplant, spinach, or flowering ferns.

7) *Hoe:* Raw fish, and in some cases, raw beef.

These dishes are always accompanied by

1) Rice
2) *Tang*—soup or casserloe
3) Vinegar-Soy Sauce
4) Soy sauce
5) Mustard
6) Kimchi—Korean pickles
7) A spoon and chopsticks

II. *Kyeot Sang*

A course served in addition to the main rice course. If the rice course is the informal seven-dish combination, this additional course is rather simple. But if the main course has nine or twelve dishes, the side course is also formal.

Foods served on this side course are:

1) *Jeonkol:* Sukiyaki of fish, beef, and beef intestines with vegetables.
2) *Banju:* Wine in a carafe, and a wine cup.
3) *Bankwa:* Fruit

III. *Myeon Sang*

Noodles served for everyday lunch. Usually accompanied by fruit, rice cakes, and drinks.

IV. *Kyoja Sang*

The most formal presentation of dishes served at celebrations or formal dinners.

V. *Juan Sang*

A special wine course at a formal table. The accompanying dishes are good as hors d'oeuvres.

VI. *Keun Sang*

The celebration table for the 61st birthday or wedding ceremonies. The ingredients are arranged in the form of a mound and are intricately decorated with artificial flowers or other ornaments to delight the eyes.

VII. *Saeng-il Sang*

The presentation to celebrate a birth. For the firstborn child there is a special decorative display at dishes that are symbolic in nature rather than edible. These include uncooked rice (symbolizing good luck); buckwheat noodles (longevity); calligraphy (family creed); *Cheon-ja-mun* (books); coins (wealth); *Daechu* (many sons); an ink stone, brushes, and an ink-stick (letters). To celebrate the birth of a son, to these things are added a bow and arrow (bravery) and a scroll (hand writing); and for a girl a scale or threads to encourage the new born child.

VIII. *Je Sang*

The dishes for the first (*So Sang*) and second (*Dae Sang*) anniversaries of a preson's death. The arrangement of this food is formal and the combination of dishes is set by a strictly observed tradition. None of the dishes in this presentation contains a single dash of hot pepper.

1) Five kinds of soup (*O-Tang*)

Yuk Tang:	Beef soup
Bong Tang:	Chicken soup
Eo Tang:	Fish soup
So Tang:	Vegetable soup
Jap Tang:	Soup containing vegetables, mushrooms, and eggs.

2) Five kinds of meat, fish or vegetables roasted or toasted (*O-Jeok*).

3) Other foods

Eo-Po:	Dried sliced fish
Dangsok:	Cube suger and ball sugar, *Ohwa Dang* and *Maehwa Dang*.
Kwasil:	An uneven number of fresh and dried fruits.
Kwajul:	Fried cookies and crackers with Korean tea.

These are accompanied by wine, rice, noodles, rice cakes and pickles.

Dinner Trays

Three kinds of trays are generally used.

1) *Nemo Sang:* A rectangular tray to serve 1 or 2

2) *Dulle Sang:* A 6-, 8-, or 12-sided tray to serve 1 or 2.

3) *Kae-ryang Sang:* A large round tray to serve many people.

Tableware

In the court tradition, silverware is used, but common people use chinaware or inexpensive brass.

In Korea rice and soup are eaten with a spoon which, once it is picked up, must not be set down on the tray again, but be left over the rice bowl or in the soup bowl. Chopsticks are used only to take food from the serving dishes and must be left on the tray each time.

Names and functions of tableware:

1)	*Jubal:*	Brass rice bowls
2)	*Sabal:*	Chine rice bowls
3)	*Bari:*	Rice bowls for women
4)	*Kongki:*	General term for rice bowls
5)	*Tangki:*	General term for soup bowls
6)	*Daejeop:*	Serving bowls for hot or cold water
7)	*Hap:*	Serving bowls for rice, rice cakes, or noodles
8)	*Jobanki:*	Bowls for the same purpose as *Hap*, but in a little different shape
9)	*Ban-byeong-ki:*	Bowls for the same purpose as *Hap*, but in a little different shape
10)	*Jongji:*	A small condiment dish for soy sauce, vinegar-soy sauce, mustard, or honey
11)	*Bosiki:*	Pickle dishes
12)	*Jeopsi:*	Serving dishes for ordinary, everyday dishes
13)	*Jochipo:*	Serving dishes for steamed foods or soup
14)	*Ju-jeon-ja:*	Wine jugs or carafes
15)	*Jaeng ban:*	Brass serving tray. A wooden one is called *Cha ban*.
16)	*Su-jeo:*	Spoons and chopsticks

The specialties are served in purposely designed dishes (for example, the 9-compartment lacquer dish, p. 56, and the fire pot, p. 49).

Index of Recipes